INSPIRING LIVES

DWIGHT HOWARD

Superman of Basketball

By Malcolm J. Harasymiw

Gareth Stevens Publishing

Please visit our Web site www.garethstevens.com. For a free color catalog of all our high-quality books, call toll free 1-800-542-2595 or fax 1-877-542-2596.

Library of Congress Cataloging-in-Publication Data

Harasymiw, Malcolm J.
Dwight Howard : superman of basketball / Malcolm J. Harasymiw.
p. cm. — (Inspiring lives)
Includes index.
ISBN 978-1-4339-3641-8 (pbk.)
ISBN 978-1-4339-3642-5 (6-pack)
ISBN 978-1-4339-3640-1 (library binding)
1. Howard, Dwight—Juvenile literature. 2. Basketball players—United States—Biography—Juvenile literature. I. Title.
GV884.H68H37 2010
796.323092—dc22
[B]

2009037274

Published in 2010 by Gareth Stevens Publishing
111 East 14th Street, Suite 349
New York, NY 10003

Designer: Daniel Hosek
Editor: Therese Shea

Photo credits: Cover, title page © Chris McGrath/Getty Images; p. 5 © Ronald Martinez/Getty Images; p. 7 © Ethan Miller/Getty Images; p. 9 © Paul Abell/WireImage/Getty Images; pp. 11, 13 © Nathaniel S. Butler/NBA/Getty Images; p. 15 © Gregory Shamus/Getty Images; p. 17 © Jonathan Daniel/Getty Images; p. 19 © Andrew D. Bernstein/NBA/Getty Images; p. 21 © Fernando Medina/NBA/Getty Images; p. 23 © Timothy A. Clary/AFP/Getty Images; p. 25 © Jesse D. Garrabrant/NBA/Getty Images; p. 27 © Bill Baptist/NBA/Getty Images; p. 29 © Mike Moore/WireImage/Getty Images.

Printed in the United States of America

CPSIA compliance information: Batch #CW10GS: For further information contact Gareth Stevens, New York, New York at 1-800-542-2595.

Contents

Number 12

Dwight Howard is one of the best players in the NBA. He is number 12 on the Orlando Magic.

MAGIC
12
ODOM

Young Dwight

Dwight was born in Atlanta, Georgia, in 1985. His father is a policeman. His mother played basketball in school.

Dwight played basketball in high school. He wanted to play in the NBA. He knew he had to practice hard.

SAHA
12
BULLDOGS
34

Dwight was named the best high school player in the United States in 2004!

12
ALL AMERICAN

The Orlando Magic

Dwight was the first player picked in the NBA draft in 2004. He was chosen by the Orlando Magic.

25

Dwight started every game with the Magic. He scored about 12 points a game.

HOWARD
12
36
ORLANDO
9

The Magic did not reach the playoffs. Dwight had to practice harder.

Becoming the Best

Dwight's practice paid off. He had the most rebounds in the NBA from 2007 to 2008.

LAKERS
LOS ANGELES LAKERS
ORLANDO
2
LAKERS
2
LAKERS
24
The only choice of the La

Dwight had the most blocks in the NBA from 2008 to 2009. He helped make the Magic into a playoff team.

Dwight learned to become a great player.

People call him "Superman"!

Golden Moments

Dwight helped the U.S. basketball team win gold medals at the 2008 Olympics.

USA
TEAM 2008

Dwight was named an All-Star in 2007, 2008, and 2009! All-Stars are the best players in the NBA.

EAST
12
WEST

Helping Others

Dwight teaches kids to play basketball.

He is a star in many ways!

JAM
SESSION

Timeline

1985 Dwight is born in Atlanta, Georgia.

2004 Dwight is named the best high school basketball player.

2004 Dwight is picked first in the NBA draft.

2007 Dwight plays in his first All-Star game.

2008 Dwight has the most rebounds in the NBA.

2008 Dwight wins a gold medal in the Olympics.

2009 Dwight has the most blocks in the NBA.

For More Information

Books:

Basen, Ryan. *Dwight Howard: Gifted and Giving Basketball Star.* Berkeley Heights, NJ: Enslow Publishers, 2010.

Fawaz, John. *Dwight Howard.* New York: Scholastic, 2010.

Hareas, John. *Basketball.* New York: DK Publishing, 2005.

Web Sites:

NBA: Dwight Howard Info Page

www.nba.com/playerfile/dwight_howard

The Official DwightHoward.com

www.dwighthoward.com

Publisher's note to educators and parents: Our editors have carefully reviewed these Web sites to ensure that they are suitable for students. Many Web sites change frequently, however, and we cannot guarantee that a site's future contents will continue to meet our high standards of quality and educational value. Be advised that students should be closely supervised whenever they access the Internet.

Glossary

draft: in sports, the system for choosing players for teams

medal: a round piece of metal given as a prize

NBA: short form of National Basketball Association

Olympics: an event of many sports contests between many countries

playoffs: a number of games that decides the winning team of a sport's season

rebound: in basketball, a ball that has bounced off the backboard or rim

Index